Childhood of Jesus

Childhood of Jesus

JEFFREY D. JOHNSON

WIPF & STOCK · Eugene, Oregon

CHILDHOOD OF JESUS

Wipf & Stock
An Imprint of Wipf and Stock Publishers
199 W. 8th Ave., Suite 3
Eugene, OR 97401
www.wipfandstock.com

ISBN 13: 978-1-61097-111-9

Manufactured in the U.S.A.

Dedicated to Hyman Appelman—a faithful erudite of Scripture. It was through his powerful teaching I came to faith in Jesus the Messiah, and to Zola Levitt whose influence on my life regarding the Jewish Roots of Christianity was nothing less than profound. Both men are in Heaven—I look forward to seeing Hyman once again and to meet Zola face to face for the first time on that great reunion day!

Childhood of Jesus

A NSELM OF Canterbury (ca. 1033–1109) commented regarding the virgin birth of the Messiah: *"Exercise your pictorial art, then, not on an empty fiction, but upon a solid truth, and say that it is extremely fitting that, as the sin of man and the cause of our condemnation took their origin from a woman, so the cure for sin and the cause of our salvation must be born of a woman. And so that women may not despair of attaining to the lot of the blessed, because such great evil has issued from a woman, it was fitting that such a great good should issue from a woman, to revitalize their hope. Add this to your painting: If it was a virgin who was the cause of all evil to the human race, it is far more fitting that it be a virgin who will be the cause of all good. Depict this also: If the woman whom God made from a man without a woman was made from a virgin, it is also extremely fitting that the man who will originate from a woman without a man be born of a virgin. But for the present, let these examples suffice of the pictures that can be depicted on the fact that the God-man must be born of a virgin woman"* (Zondervan 1996: 1176).

Not much is recorded for us in the New Testament about the life of Jesus between his birth and the scene where he is in the Temple talking with the scholars, nor is there much written about his life between his time in the Temple and the beginning of his ministry at the age of 30. What was he doing during those "silent years?"

As one looks at the record, according to Scripture, of the Lord's life and teaching, you will find a Jewish cultural distinctive. You will find a deep commitment to the Jewish customs and beliefs of his day. Jesus grew up in a Jewish family setting. His parents observed Jewish Law and religious practices. Jesus would have celebrated all the Jewish holidays. He would have been faithful in observing the Sabbath, regularly attending synagogue as well as being exposed to rabbinical teaching and expectations (Matthew 1; Luke 2; Luke 4).

Some believe that Jesus was not educated, due to a few verses such as "'Can any good thing come out of Nazareth?' And they were all amazed and marveled, saying, ' . . . Are not all these which speak Galileans?' And the [religious] Jews marveled, saying, 'How does this man know letters, having never studied?'" (John 1:46; Acts 2:7; John 7:15). These statements reflected a tension and intolerance between Judea and Galilee. Those in Judea saw themselves as being more sophisticated than their Galilean counterparts. They saw the Galileans as being backward and ignorant. When a Judean heard a Galilean speak, they heard a dolt's voice.

The truth of the matter, according to Shmuel Safrai, Hebrew University Professor of Jewish History of the Mishnaic and Talmudic Periods, stated, "Not only do the number of first-century Galilean sages exceed the number of Judean sages, but the moral and ethical quality of their teaching is still considered more highly than that of their Judean counterparts" (Bivin 1993).

Galilee would have been the conservative religious and political bastion of Israel. Anticipation for the advent of Messiah was very high in this region. Now, with this background in mind, let's consider Luke's account of Jesus' childhood in Luke 2:40–52 and draw some conclusions.

Luke 2:40–52
Family History

The Scripture does not record for us exactly what Jesus did between the age of 12 and the beginning of his public ministry at the age of 30; however, John does tell us that *"the world itself could not contain the books that would be written"* about the Lord's life (John 21:25). There are apocryphal writings, extra-biblical attempts to record so-called events in the life of Jesus. Stories include Jesus traveling to India to study yoga and Jesus, as a little boy in Egypt, making clay pigeons, touching them causing them to fly, as well as Jesus having an encounter with E. T.

The New Testament records for us that people knew Jesus, where he lived as well as who his parents were (Mat. 13:55; Mk. 6:3). Jesus grew up in a typical Jewish home, the son of a carpenter.

Shortly after Jesus was born, Joseph took Mary and two-year-old Jesus to Egypt because Herod ordered the children in Bethlehem slaughtered. Early Christians believed this was a fulfillment of Rachel weeping for her children, as found in Jeremiah 31:15. How long the family lived in Egypt, we do not know; however, we do know that when they came back, they settled in Nazareth (Matt. 2:19–23).

Luke records for us a brief sketch in the life of Jesus as a child being twelve years old (Luke 2:40) : "And the Child grew and became strong in spirit, filled with wisdom; and the grace of God was upon him." The word "grew" (Gr. Auxano) is a term that implies a physical growth. The Hebrew equivalent is *tsemach*, which means "a tender shoot or plant," or the Hebrew word gadel, which means "becoming great." "Child" means half-grown boy or girl. Luke was simply telling us that Jesus grew up like any other little Jewish boy with no great responsibility except to parental and religious authority.

Luke continues and states in 2:52, "And Jesus increased in wisdom and stature, and in favor with God and men." The word "increased" means to be fruitful, to drive forward (through discipline), to advance. Within the context of verse 40, we have the description of Jesus growing up as a child before the age of 12. Arriving at verse 52, we find a description of Jesus as an adolescent through adulthood growing (increasing) mentally, physically, and spiritually.

Luke reveals events that occurred between Christ's birth and adolescence in verses 41–46: "His parents went to Jerusalem every year at the Feast of the Passover. And when he was twelve years old, they went up to Jerusalem according to the custom of the feast. When they had finished the days, as they returned, the boy Jesus lingered behind in Jerusalem. And Joseph and his mother did not know it; but supposing him to have been in the company, they went a day's journey, and sought him among their relatives and acquaintances. So when they did not find him they returned to Jerusalem, seeking him. Now so it was that after three days they found him in the temple, sitting in the midst of the teachers both listening to them and asking them questions."

Three days refer to traveling away from the city one day; traveling back to the city one day; and another day to find him. The questioning and answering is called putting sh'eilot and was an intense dialogue between twelve-year-old Jesus and some of the greatest minds of Biblical Judaism. Some believe this was the prototype of what would eventually become the bar mitzvah.

Luke then records the reaction of the scholars regarding this little boy in verse 47: "And all who heard him were astonished at his understanding and answers." These scholars were dazed by the treatise coming from this child. However, apparently this did not impress Mary and Joseph. "So when they saw him, they were amazed; and his mother said to him, 'Son, why have you done this to us? Look, your father and I have sought you anxiously'" (verse 48).

Normally, a Jewish woman would never barge in, breaking up a conversation of the sages as boldly as Mary did. Nevertheless, she was a mother and her son was missing . . . and now He was found. Notice her words: "Son"—a mixture of anger, relief, fear, joy. "Your father and I" is a very typical response for parents in a crisis moment that has been met with relief. As parents, Mary and Joseph were very anxious over Jesus' safety, as there would have been a great infusion of people in Jerusalem for the Passover. Some suggest over a million visitors would have traveled to Jerusalem. A little boy could get lost in such a crowd.

At this intense moment, Luke records for us a theological conundrum: "And he said to them, 'Why did you seek me: Did you not know that I must be about my Father's business?" In this stage of his life, what was his Father's will (referring to his heavenly Father, not Joseph)? An assumed answer is found in the next verse: "Then he went down with them and came to Nazareth, and was subject to them, but his mother kept all these things in her heart" (verse 51). Therefore, as a teenager, Jesus would have remained "subject" to his earthly parents.

For Luke to know all these details, according to tradition, suggests that Mary may have told him her story, thus Luke would have learned these facts firsthand from the mother of Jesus.

Basically, according to the text, we have a little Jewish boy living in Nazareth, helping his father around the carpenter's shop, running errands, fetching water in Nazareth for Mary, and playing. According to tradition, sometime in Jesus' late teens or early twenties, Joseph died, which would have had a profound impact on the family economically, socially, and emotionally.

Homework for Jesus

Education would have been important to Joseph and Mary. Two thousand years ago, Jewish parents would give their four- or five-year-old child a honey cake with Psalm 119:103 inscribed on it. *"How sweet are your words to my taste, sweeter than honey to my mouth."* This would have been one of the child's first lessons on the goodness of the Word of God. It is sweet to the taste. It is good for you.

From the Mishnah (Avot 5:21), we read a passage regarding the life stages of a Jewish child: "At 5 years of age, one is ready for the study of the written Torah, at 10 years of age the study of the Oral Torah, at 13 for bar mitzvah, at 15 for the study of halachot (rabbinic legal decisions), at 18 for marriage, at 20 for pursuing a vocation, at 30 for entering one's full vigor"(Biven, 1993). Education was highly esteemed and valued in Jewish society. In Against Apion 1:60, Josephus stated, "Above all we pride ourselves on the education of our children, and regard as the most essential task in life the observance of our laws and of the pious practices based thereupon, which we have inherited" (Biven, 1993).

Synagogues in the first century usually had their own school called Bet Sefer, which is an elementary school, or Bet Midrash, a secondary school. Along with the children, adults would study the Scripture and tradition. The formal educational process ended at the age of 13, when most of the young people would go to work. A few good students would continue with part-time studies and working a part-time job. A few exceptional students would leave home and study with a famous rabbi as their families supported them. The Apostle Paul, an exceptional student, experienced such an education with the famous teacher Gamaliel.

The Babylonian Talmud, Shabbat 30a, states, "Study is one of the highest forms of worship." The Mishnah, Avot 2:12, says, "Discipline yourself to study Torah, for you do not acquire it by inheritance" (Biven, 1993). These texts remind us of the Jews at Berea who "were more noble . . . and searched the scriptures daily, whether those things were so" (Acts 17:11). These sayings were probably the motivational impetus behinds Paul's statement, "Study to shew thyself approved unto God, a workman that needeth not to be ashamed, rightly dividing the Word of truth" (2 Tim. 2:15). Peter declared, "Giving all diligence, add to your faith, virtue, and to virtue knowledge" (2 Pet. 1:5).

To own a copy of the scriptures, or a Torah scroll, would have been difficult for the common person at the time of Jesus, as it would have been very expensive to own. Therefore, very few families had copies of the scrolls. As a result, a lot of memorization had to take place. Shmuel Safrai stated that "[t]here is the frequent expression, 'the chirping of children,' which was heard by people passing close by a synagogue as the children were reciting a verse. Adults too, in individual and group study, often read aloud; for it was frequently advised not to learn in a whisper, but aloud. This was the only way to overcome the danger of forgetting" (The Jewish People in the First Century, Vol. 2, p. 953; Biven, 1993).

The sages believed that repetition was very important to learning. "A person who repeats his lesson a hundred times is not to be compared with him who repeats it a hundred and one times" (Babylonian Talmud, Hagigah 9b). "If [the students] learn Torah and does not go over it again and again, he is like a man who sows without reaping" (Babylonian Talmud, Sanhedrin 99a). If students memorized outdoors, they often could be distracted by the beautiful scenery; therefore, the Mishnah states that " person walking along the road repeating his lessons who interrupts his memorization and exclaims: 'What a beautiful tree!' or 'What a beautiful field!' it is imputed to him as if he were guilty of a crime punishable by death." (Avot 3:8; Biven, 1993). Education ,therefore, was very important to the first-century family, and Jesus would have been exposed to the best possible training the family could muster.

CHILDHOOD OF JESUS

We just covered the New Testament account of the childhood of Jesus and looked at early Christian thought about Jesus' birth, briefly skimming over early Hebraic impulses about Jewish life two thousand years ago. Now let's take it one step further and look at a mystical psalm that pulls back a curtain, allowing us to peek at the Holy Family living in Nazareth.

Psalm 69

Mystical Words

Psalm 69 is a mystical a messianic psalm. Yes, David was writing of his personal experience and challenges, and yet he wrote of the woes of another yet to come. This psalm is one of the most quoted psalms in the New Testament, as it refers to the Messiah. This poetic portrait is a presage to be sure, mysterious in context and mystical in expounding profound spiritual insights. It takes us behind the scenes, revealing the childhood of Messiah, the One who was foretold to come. We discover the personal pain Jesus experienced as a little boy, a precursor of things to come when he was an adult. The psalm was written approximately 900 years before Mary gave birth to her firstborn son. Let's take a look at this marvelous exposé of the childhood of Jesus.

VERSES 1–4

He didn't do it; however, he must fix it

"Save me, O God! For the waters have come up to my neck. I sink in deep mire, where there is no standing; I have come into deep waters, where the floods overflow me. My throat is dry; my eyes fail while I wait for my God. Those who hate me without a cause are more than the hairs of my head; they are mighty who would destroy me, being my enemies wrongfully; though I have stolen nothing, I still must restore it."

These verses reveal to us one who is wrongfully accused, with multitudes hating him without cause. He must restore that which he did not take. These factors are clearly a reference to the cross and redemption that comes through the shed blood of the Lamb, a restoring of the soul's relationship that has been severed because of sin. We also see an inference to the crying of a boy or a young child experiencing distress or anguish.

VERSE 7

Suffering Lamb

"Because for your sake I have borne reproach; shame has covered my face."

Verse seven is another clear reference to Messiah as the suffering Lamb of God. Jesus, the One who would stand before the officials of Jerusalem, hearing the crowd's false accusations and experiencing the full thrust of Rome's judicial power. Jesus' teaching moved the masses and upset the religious order. That day, in the place where the Glory of God abode in the Holy of Holies, Jesus, the incarnate God, was about to endure the history's most grueling punishment of all: the cross. He was innocent, yet he bore our reproach and shame.

VERSES 8 AND 9

Bastard Son

"I have become a stranger to my brothers, and an alien to my mother's children; because zeal for your house has eaten me up, and the reproaches of those who reproach you have fallen on me."

Not only do these verses speak of the rejection of Jesus by the religious leaders of his day, but also his disciples, who fled from his side when the Roman soldiers came to take Jesus away, led by Judas Iscariot. And yet, there is another level of interpretation, referencing his siblings as he was growing up who did not believe until after the resurrection.

Nazareth was a little town of around 200 people in the time of Jesus. The townspeople found it difficult to accept Jesus and to believe that he was the son of God (Prov. 30:4; John 2:17; Luke 8:19; Romans 15:3). There would have been a lot of gossip about Mary. The talk about town would have gone something like this:

"Joseph was not the Father. They said it was an angel that appeared to her and announced she was pregnant. Can you believe it?"

This kind of talk would have been emphasized in Mark 6:3, where Jesus taught in his hometown synagogue and the congregants who knew Jesus made these comments: "Is this not the carpenter, the Son of Mary . . . ?" First of all, in ancient Jewish culture, a son was never identified through his mother, only through his father. Jesus should have been addressed as Yeshua ben Yossi, or Jesus son of Joseph. By referencing him as Yeshua ben Mariam, or son of Mary, they were calling him a bastard son, or directly insulting Mary as a loose woman of low morals. Jesus was simply not accepted in his hometown and would have been considered a bastard son.

His younger siblings would have been affected by the peer pressure of the townspeople. There would have been an immeasurable amount of tension between family members and the community.

VERSES 11 AND 12

Ridiculed by Neighbors

"I also made sackcloth my garment; I became a byword to them. Those who sit in the gate speak against me, and I am the song of the drunkards."

Sackcloth is a symbol of a servant, also associated with guilt. Jesus, being God-Man bore the guilt of our sin on the cross. Some believe that sackcloth was used on the one crucified in order to fasten him more securely on the cross.

Jesus, growing up and being a citizen of Nazareth, would have been ridiculed by the neighbors to the point of becoming a slanderous byword, a proverb, at the places of important dialogue within the community. The elders, rulers, judges, or officials who sat at the gate of the city of Nazareth would have talked about Mary and Joseph and their "situation" with Jesus.

The drunkards may refer to those in Nazareth as he was growing up or to those in Jerusalem during the Passover celebration after drinking wine. Perhaps the psalmist was also referring to the soldiers who may have drunk the spiced wine used to dull the senses of those on the cross and substituted it with vinegar. Nevertheless, you get the picture.

VERSES 19, 20, AND 21

Heavy Heart

"You know my reproach, my shame, and my dishonor; my adversaries are all before you. Reproach has broken my heart, and I am full of heaviness; I looked for someone to take pity, but there was none; and for comforters, but I found none. They also gave me gall for my food, and for my thirst they gave me vinegar to drink."

The Lord manifested compassion on those who hated him, who made fun of him, who made his name a byword from an early age. As a child, his heart became so heavy looking for someone to take pity and found none who would. Moments like these would have prepared Jesus, as a small-town boy, for the eventual challenge of facing adversaries in the Roman courts, ultimately leading up to his execution in the years to come, and while hanging on the cross between heaven and earth, dying for something he did not do, he was able to say, "Father forgive them for they know not what they do" (Luke 23:34).

Gall and vinegar are clear references to the cross as they attempted to give the Lord this gall (a sedative pain reliever) and sour wine to drink, but he refused it (Matthew 27:34, 48; Mark 15:23; Luke 23:36; John 19:29).

VERSE 26

Smitten

"For they persecute him whom thou hast smitten; and they talk to the grief of those whom thou hast wounded."

We are reminded of the Isaiah's words about the Messiah and the reason for this prophetic chapter: Jesus "shall grow up . . . despised and rejected . . . a man of sorrows and acquainted with grief . . ." persecuted, "smitten of God and afflicted . . . Yet it pleased the Lord to bruise him, he has put him to grief . . . He was numbered with the transgressors, and he bore the sin of many and made intercession for the transgressors" (53:3–5, 10, 12). Also, Zechariah stated, "Strike the shepherd, and the sheep will be scattered" (13:7).

We discover within the texts of the prophets that God orchestrated all the events regarding the life and childhood of Jesus leading up the death, burial, and resurrection.

So, in the final analysis:

1. Jesus was imperiled at birth as Herod tried to kill him.

2. He was an alien in Egypt as a child.

3. He was made slanderous byword (made fun of) and gossiped about in his hometown.

4. He was misunderstood by his siblings and peers.

5. His mother was ridiculed with gossip from the town's people questioning her morals.

6. Jesus' earthly Father died at a most crucial time when a young man needs his dad.

7. As an adult, Jesus was rejected, abused, and ultimately crucified.

Why?

Why would the infinite, eternal God go to such length to create human beings only to have them resist the one who gave them life? Why would the all-powerful God choose to reveal himself through the passage of a virgin's womb, becoming a little boy? Why would the all-knowing God want this manifestation of himself become part of a tribe of people that is so misunderstood? Why would he subject himself to the brutality of a horrible execution? Why would God reveal his essence this way?

"Seeing then that we have a great High Priest who has passed through the heavens, Jesus the Son of God, let us hold fast our confession. For we do not have a High Priest who cannot sympathize with our weaknesses, but was in all points tempted as we are, yet without sin. Let us therefore come boldly to the throne of grace, that we may obtain mercy and find grace to help in time of need" (Hebrews 4:14–16).

The infinite, eternal Son became flesh so we might understand. He experienced every human trial and testing. Therefore, he does understand our need; he does understand our fear; he does understand you! Will you trust the One who can give hope, comfort, peace, and eternal life?

Selected Bibliography

Bible Classics Devotional Bible, New International Version, Zondervan, 1996

Biven, David, Dispatch From Jerusalem, July/August 1993, Volume 18, Number 2

Gaer, Joseph & Wolf, Alfred,Our Jewish Heritage, Wilshire Book Co. Hollywood, CA, 1967 Edition

McGee, J. Vernon, The Message of the Silent Years, Thru the Bible Books, Pasadena, CA, 1983

Neale, Jospeh, Commentary on the Psalms, Volume 2, Masters, New York, 1868

Spurgeon, The Treasury of David, Volume 1, Thomas Nelson, Inc., Publishers

Stern, Jewish New Testament Commentary, Jewish New Testament Publications, Inc., 1992

The Holy Bible, King James Version

The Holy Bible, The New King James Version, Broadman & Holman Publishers, 1996 (all scripture used is from the NKJV, or the King James Version of the Holy Bible

Walvoord & Zuck, Bible Knowledge Commentary Old & New Testament, Victor Books, 1985

Whiston, William, Josephus Complete Works, Kregel Publications, Grand Rapids, MI, 1978

Wilson, Marvin, Our Father Abraham, Eerdmans Pubishers, Grand Rapids, MI, 1989

The lecture in this book was prepared during many weeks in a very busy and active pastorate. This paper is not for scholars and exegetes, but for plain people. No claim is made for originality, but the writer is deeply grateful for the help he received from many sources, including the above bibliography.